TARA'S
10 Tips
For
Friends
with
Autism

This book is dedicated to my brother Nate and his walk with Autism.

Tip# 1

If your friend with Autism is pacing around, take them for a walk and they will slow down.

Sensory help

Tip#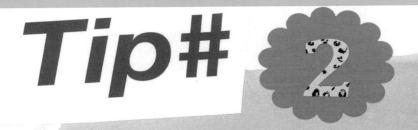

Make sure your friend has a water bottle to carry around. If they get thirsty or hot—give them something to drink on the spot.

Self-Regulation

Tip# 3

Your friend may have a stuffed toy they carry around. You can make conversation by including their toy. You might every try a puppet to friend their toy.

Socialization

Tip# 4

A friend may have a weighted vest or weighted blanket. They may also have a bean bag chair in their class.
You can offer them a book and sit in their corner with their blanket and chair. You will find friendship there.

Self-calmimg

Tip# 5

If you're at a place where there is lots of loud sounds, take your friend outside to quiet down. If you know ahead of time you're going to a loud place, head phone or ear plugs are a good thing to take.

Sensory Overload

Tip# 6

If your friend starts to cry and you want to give them a hug, stop in place. Instead of a hug your friend will want some space.

Social Distance

Tip# 7

Keep the tone of your voice soft. Avoid yelling around your friend with Autism.

Auditory Sensory

Tip# 8

Your friend with Autism has to follow the rules too. They may have a behavior plan that your can participate in too.

Behavior Plan

Positive

Behavior

Support

Quiet voice inside.

Walking feet.

Raise your hand to talk.

Tip# 9

If your friend wants a hug and you don't know what to do—a simple fist bump should do.

Social-Behavior

Tip# 10

The most important rule of all—friends with Autism are good friends too!

Friendship

Created By
By
TARA

Made in the USA
Columbia, SC
03 December 2024

47161240R00015